JENNA ORTEGA

A Little Golden Book® Biography

By Heather E. Schwartz • Illustrated by Luz Tapia

A GOLDEN BOOK • NEW YORK

Golden Books
An imprint of Random House Children's Books
A division of Penguin Random House LLC
1745 Broadway, New York, NY 10019
penguinrandomhouse.com
rhcbooks.com

Library of Congress Control Number: 2025934106
ISBN 979-8-217-12054-3 (trade) — ISBN 979-8-217-12055-0 (ebook)
Manufactured in the United States of America
10 9 8 7 6 5 4 3 2 1
EU Contact: Penguin Random House Ireland, 32 Nassau Street, Dublin D02 YH68.
https://eu-contact.penguin.ie

HAPPY

Jenna Marie Ortega was born on September 27, 2002. Her mother is Mexican and Puerto Rican. Her father is Mexican American. She grew up in California's Coachella Valley, with five siblings. Jenna is a proud Latina. She loved celebrating birthdays with piñatas and holidays with homemade Hispanic treats.

Most of Jenna's family was shy—but not Jenna! She was loud and outgoing. By age six, she decided she wanted to be an actor. Her parents didn't know if they liked that idea, but Jenna kept insisting.

Finally, her mom bought her a book of dramatic scenes to practice. She filmed Jenna performing one of the monologues and put it on social media just for fun. A casting agent saw it and thought Jenna could be a star. Jenna thought so, too! She told her family she was going to be on the Disney Channel one day.

When Jenna was nine years old, her mom drove her to Los Angeles to audition for a Colgate toothpaste commercial. She got the part!

Jenna was a natural. She appeared in many other ads, including three for McDonald's. After a year of acting in commercials, she started to audition for TV and movies.

Jenna appeared in an episode of a TV show called *Rob* in 2012. She was excited to work with the actor Cheech Marin. Jenna knew him as one half of the comedy duo Cheech & Chong. She and her dad were huge fans.

In 2014, Jenna got a recurring role on the series *Jane the Virgin*. She played the title character's younger self in thirty episodes.

At age thirteen, Jenna accomplished her goal and made it to the Disney Channel! She played Harley Diaz, the star of *Stuck in the Middle*. The comedy was about a large Hispanic family, a lot like her own.

Jenna's new job meant leaving her eighth-grade class behind. Monday through Friday, she lived, worked, and was homeschooled in Los Angeles. On weekends, she went home to see her family and friends.

Having a hit show meant people were interested in whatever Jenna did and said. So she started to speak up about important causes. She joined DoSomething.org's Pride Over Prejudice campaign to declare her pride for her family's heritage. It was a way to fight back against racial discrimination.

Disney kept Jenna busy with many exciting projects. She was the voice of a Latina princess named Isabel in the animated TV series *Elena of Avalor*. And she had her own weekly talk show on Radio Disney called *What's Good with Jenna Ortega*. It was all about spreading love and positive vibes.

Jenna was a Disney superstar. But when she went home, she was a regular kid. She played soccer and had dishes and yardwork to do. Her brothers and sisters made sure she did extra chores to make up for missing her turn. She didn't mind!

Jenna was never too busy to help others. In honor of her grandfather who died of AIDS, she worked with an organization called UNAIDS to raise awareness about the disease. She also traveled to Kenya with the WE organization to help build schools and wells, so people could have clean water to drink.

When *Stuck in the Middle* ended, Jenna was sixteen and excited to book new acting jobs. It wasn't easy. Many casting directors assumed she could only handle roles like the ones she did for Disney.

But Jenna has proven she's talented enough to do all kinds of roles. In the family adventure film *Saving Flora*, she played a girl who saves a circus elephant. In the comedy *Yes Day*, she played a teen taking charge of the family's fun. She has also been in many horror movies. Acting in them is a lot less scary than watching them!

When Jenna was seventeen, she explored a new way of expressing herself—she wrote a book! *It's All Love: Reflections for Your Heart & Soul* was full of personal stories and thoughts that she hoped could help other people.

In 2021, Jenna was asked to be part of a new Netflix series. It was based on a creepy, kooky family originally created by cartoonist Charles Addams in 1938. In the 1960s, *The Addams Family* was a funny TV show. And in 1991, it was a popular movie, with actor Christina Ricci playing the daughter of the family, Wednesday Addams.

The new show would be called *Wednesday*, and Jenna would be the star. How could she say no?

She couldn't! She got right to work to prepare for the role. Jenna studied German and learned to fence, canoe, and play cello. She even taught herself how to stare for a long time without blinking!

Jenna enjoyed coming up with ways to make her version of Wednesday unique. In one memorable scene, she did unusual dance moves while staring intensely the whole time. Fans loved it!

She was honored with the Rising Star Award for Television at the Critics Choice Association's Celebration of Latino Cinema and TV. And *Wednesday* received twelve Emmy nominations, including one for Jenna's acting, making her the third—and youngest—Latina to be nominated for Outstanding Lead Actress in a Comedy!

Jenna has been invited on lots of talk shows. She impressed the host of *Hot Ones* by how easily she ate all the spicy chicken wings. A lot in Jenna's life has changed since she started acting, but she still has her appetite for hot, spicy foods.

Soon, Jenna was back on the big screen playing Astrid in *Beetlejuice Beetlejuice*, the sequel to the 1988 movie *Beetlejuice*.

When work began on season two of *Wednesday*, Jenna had two jobs. She was an actor *and* a producer! That meant she had more control over the script, the wardrobe, and the plans for the show.

And what are Jenna's plans for her future? More acting, producing, and hopefully directing, too. She also loves music and would like to compose a film score someday.

Since she was six years old, Jenna Ortega knew she belonged on TV and in movies—and she was right!